PROTECTING

the EARTH'S

ANIMALS

Dogs and Cats

Saving Our Precious Pets

BETH ADELMAN

PROTECTING *the* **EARTH'S ANIMALS**

Dogs and Cats

Saving Our Precious Pets

BY BETH ADELMAN

Mason Crest
450 Parkway Drive, Suite D
Broomall, PA 19008
www.masoncrest.com

© 2018 by Mason Crest, an imprint of National Highlights, Inc.

Printed and bound in the United States of America.

Series ISBN: 978-1-4222-3872-1
Hardback ISBN: 978-1-4222-3875-2
EBook ISBN: 978-1-4222-7912-0

First printing
1 3 5 7 9 8 6 4 2

Produced by Shoreline Publishing Group LLC
Santa Barbara, California
Editorial Director: James Buckley Jr.
Designer: Patty Kelley
www.shorelinepublishing.com

Library of Congress Cataloging-in-Publication Data on file with the Publisher.

Cover photographs by Dreamstime.com: Verastuchelova (top); Shutterstock: Niderlander (bottom)

QR Codes disclaimer:

CONTENTS

KEY ICONS TO LOOK FOR

Words to Understand: These words with their easy-to-understand definitions will increase the reader's understanding of the text, while building vocabulary skills.

Sidebars: This boxed material within the main text allows readers to build knowledge, gain insights, explore possibilities, and broaden their perspectives by weaving together additional information to provide realistic and holistic perspectives.

Educational Videos: Readers can view videos by scanning our QR codes, providing them with additional educational content to supplement the text. Examples include news coverage, moments in history, speeches, iconic moments, and much more!

Text-Dependent Questions: These questions send the reader back to the text for more careful attention to the evidence presented here.

Research Projects: Readers are pointed toward areas of further inquiry connected to each chapter. Suggestions are provided for projects that encourage deeper research and analysis.

Series Glossary of Key Terms: This back-of-the-book glossary contains terminology used throughout this series. Words found here increase the reader's ability to read and comprehend higher-level books and articles in this field.

INTRODUCTION

It wasn't so long ago that cats and dogs lived outside, in our backyards and garages and barns. They had jobs to do—herd the sheep, protect the house, hunt the mice. Those jobs did not include sitting on the couch with us while we watched TV or hanging out on our desk while we did our homework.

Things have really changed for our pets! Most cats and dogs live inside our homes and apartments with us now. If a dog has an outside doghouse, it might be like a mini mansion. And he'll still get to come inside with his people. Even cats who roam around the neighborhood usually have a cat door so they can come and go; mostly you see them lounging in the sun on their windowsills. They live with us, as part of the family.

Cats and dogs are by far the most popular pets in America. Nobody knows exactly how many pet cats and dogs there are, but there are some good estimates. The American Pet Products Association (APPA) says there are about 78 million pet dogs and 86 million pet cats in the United States. Americans spent about $62.75 billion on their pets

Cats are the most popular pet animal in the United States.

in 2016, on everything from food and toys and furniture to veterinarian visits and pet sitters.

It seems like dogs and cats are living the good life. But are we killing them with kindness? Obesity is quickly becoming the number one health problem of cats and dogs. Not far behind is boredom, which leads to all kinds of behavior problems—from aggression toward their people to self-destructive behaviors—and some health problems as well. And are there too many dogs and cats out there? Is overpopulation a big problem?

It's not enough to pamper our dogs and cats; we also need to understand them. When we learn about their natural behaviors, it helps us better understand what they need to be happy and healthy living with us.

WORDS TO UNDERSTAND

euthanize   gently and humanely put to death

feral   an animal of a domesticated species who is born in the wild

neuter   a surgical procedure that makes it impossible for a male animal to father babies

rehome   find a new home for

spay   a surgical procedure that makes it impossible for a female animal to have babies

HOMELESS CATS AND DOGS

Do we have too many cats and dogs? The American Pet Products Association (APPA) says about 54 million American households own dogs and about 43 million have cats. With 86 million cats and dogs in all, that works out to an average of two cats per household, or 1.43 dogs. (Remember, that's an average; nobody actually has 1.43 dogs!)

Certainly, every family should have as many pets as they want and can take good care of. That means enough space, enough time, and enough money. People who have several cats or dogs—or birds or fish or hamsters or guinea pigs—and are taking good care of all of them are not a problem. The problem is homeless animals—animals who live in parking lots and alleys and abandoned buildings, with no place to go home to—and animals who end up in shelters and rescue groups.

Overcrowded Shelters

According to the ASPCA, about 7.6 million companion animals enter animal shelters nationwide every year. Of those, about 3.9 million are dogs and 3.4 million are cats. About two-thirds of all the dogs who enter a shelter are either returned to their owners or adopted, but less than half of all cats are.

The people at animal shelters work hard to take care of the companion animals in their care and **rehome** them. They sponsor adoption fairs and other events to encourage people to meet their residents and give a homeless pet a new forever home. But most shelters don't have enough space, enough resources, and enough forever homes to take care of all the animals that are brought to them. What happens then?

Most shelters are part of a citywide or regional network of animal rescue groups. These groups will go into a shelter and take pets they think they can rehome. There are rescue groups for specific breeds of dogs and cats, for example,

Many rabbits are returned to shelters after being given as gifts.

or for just one species, such as cats or rabbits or parrots. Many rescue groups take dogs or cats of all types. Sometimes the rescue group has a shelter building, and sometimes it's just a network of volunteers who take care of the dogs and cats in their homes until they are adopted.

But not all dogs and cats will find their way to rescue groups and, eventually, new homes. Some shelters have a contract with the city or county where they are located. The contracts say that they must take in every animal brought to them. That means when all the places for cats or dogs are filled, if someone brings in another cat or dog, room must be made for that animal. Shelters make room by sending some animals to other rescue groups. But there are not enough places in rescue groups for every homeless dog or cat. So shelters also make room by **euthanizing** a cat or dog that is unlikely to be adopted.

Sometimes these are animals with health problems such as arthritis, diabetes, asthma or digestive issues that will need ongoing care. Sometimes they're animals with behavior problems, such as aggression or soiling in the house or shyness. Sometimes they're just older animals; people are more likely to adopt puppies and kittens, so the older animals can be hard to rehome.

Unfortunately, the majority of cats and dogs euthanized in shelters have no problems and would make great pets,

Shelter animals rarely get much freedom to roam around.

but they have just been there a long time and the shelter needs to make room for more animals coming in. Of all the animals that end up in shelters, 31 percent of all the dogs and 41 percent of all cats are euthanized, according to the American Society for the Prevention of Cruelty to Animals (ASPCA).

Some shelters—typically those that do not rely on any public funding—are no-kill, meaning they keep all the animals brought to them until they can find homes for them. When these groups are full, they just don't accept any more pets. Some no-kill shelters may also put limitations on the pets they accept—no animals over a certain age, or no animals with health or behavior problems, for example. Their resources are limited, and they want to use them to rehome as many animals as possible, so they don't take in animals that are less likely to be adopted.

Being kept in a cage can have long-term harmful effects.

No one knows for sure how many animals are eutha-

COMMUNITY CATS

Community cats live outside in groups they have formed themselves. They usually gather around a source of food, such as behind a restaurant or near a supermarket, or in areas where they can catch mice or rats. The HSUS estimates there may be 30 to 40 million community cats in America. While some have gotten away from their homes or have been dumped by their owners, most are **feral**.

It is terrifying for a pet cat to be dumped in a cat community. Cats who are used to living in a home don't do well

and dogs are on the move all the time, being sent to the places where they are most likely to find forever homes.

One city's shelter story

Breed Bans

A controversial way that some governments are trying to reduce dog populations is breed-specific legislation (BSL). This includes laws that target certain types of dogs that people in the community have decided are dangerous. The laws may put restrictions on the dogs, such as that they must wear a muzzle in public, or they may ban the breed entirely. Breeds labeled as "dangerous" in this type of legislation commonly include Pit Bull-type dogs (dogs with a "pit bull look"), as well as the American Pit Bull Terrier, American Staffordshire Terrier, Staffordshire Bull Terrier, and Bull Terrier. Often other breeds are included, such as Rottweilers, Doberman Pinschers, and Bullmastiffs.

Municipalities usually pass these laws in response to serious attacks by dogs. But there are many problems with BSL. First of all, several studies have shown that even people very familiar with dog breeds cannot reliably determine what mix of breeds a mixed-breed dog is. Dogs are often incorrectly classified as Pit Bulls based solely on their looks.

Pit bulls are often targeted by municipal "breed bans."

BSL also does not take a dog's actual behavior into account, or even his genetics, so dogs who simply look like one of the targeted breeds are labeled "dangerous." By saying that all dogs who look a certain way are dangerous causes innocent dogs to suffer and perhaps even to be euthanized without evidence that they pose a threat. Responsible dog owners are forced to give up their dogs or move.

The evidence also shows that BSL does not protect communities from dangerous dogs. Studies from cities around the world show that the number and severity of dog bites do not go down as a result of BSL. So cities and states spend their efforts enforcing restrictions and bans that don't work, instead of putting that effort into establishing and strictly enforcing licensing, leash, and dogfighting laws, and targeting owners of dogs who pose a real risk to the community.

TEXT-DEPENDENT QUESTIONS

1. What does rehome mean?

2. What does the text say about the change in the number of dogs and cats being euthanized?

3. What is a community cat?

RESEARCH PROJECT

Locate an animal shelter in your area and read about their rules for accepting animals. Make a poster encouraging people to adopt animals from that shelter.

 WORDS TO UNDERSTAND

brachycephalic having a broad, short skull and a flat face

breed standard an official description of what the ideal example of each breed should be like

cesarean section a surgical method of giving birth

gene pool the available supply of different genes in a population

genetic diversity the extent to which the genes in a gene pool come from different individuals

outcross mate an animal of one breed to an animal of a different breed

MUDDYING THE GENE POOL

In July of 2016, the British Veterinary Association issued a statement calling on breeders of **brachycephalic** dog breeds to change the way these dogs are bred. The idea was to "ensure high-risk breeds, such as the English Bulldog, do not continue to suffer unnecessarily." They suggested revising the **breed standard** to add limits on features such as the shortness of the muzzle, and to consider breeding Bulldogs to dogs of different breeds, to reduce the chances of puppies inheriting genetic disorders.

Why was the statement necessary? Because people were breeding dogs to have specific traits and that process was becoming dangerous. A study published in the scientific journal *Canine Genetics and Epidemiology* looked at the **genetic diversity** of 102 English Bulldogs. The researchers found that the same concentrations of genes that produced the dog's exaggerated features also produced problems with the immune system and other serious health problems. Simply breeding dogs with longer muzzles and smaller heads would not fix the problems caused by having such a small **gene pool**.

Just three months earlier, in April 2016, *Canine Genetics and Epidemiology* published another study that looked at the weight, height, and skull shape of 180 dog breeds from Australia, and how popularity trends have changed from

Pugs' health can be negatively affected by breeding practices.

1986 to 2013. They found that dogs with extremely wide faces and short bodies, such as Pugs, Bulldogs, Shih Tzu, French Bulldogs, and Boxers, have grown more and more popular. But, the researchers said, these brachycephalic breeds often have breathing difficulties, skin disorders, overheating, dental problems, and eye conditions that are caused by their exaggerated shape. "These dogs are dying, we think, four years earlier than dogs of the same size with normal-shaped skulls," said Dr. Paul McGreevy, one of the researchers.

These studies highlighted two problems that seem to be getting worse for dog breeds—and cat breeds, too. The first is the way humans are choosing to exaggerate the characteristics of many breeds, so that the physical shape of the animal causes health problems. And the second is the very limited gene pool that concentrates any genetic flaws a breed may have.

Exaggerating the Differences

If you look at old paintings and photographs of many dog breeds, and even some cat breeds, you'll see that they look quite different from today. In the old pictures, all the brachycephalic breeds had smaller heads, longer muzzles,

CHOPPING OFF EARS AND TAILS

Several breeds of dogs in the United States that have naturally floppy ears are typically shown in dog shows with a part of their ear flaps cut off, so their ears stand up. This is called cropping. Some breeds that are usually shown with cropped ears include Boxers, Great Danes, Schnauzers, Doberman Pinschers, and Boston Terriers.

The earflaps are cut off when the dog is a puppy. The ears are then taped to stiff supports to help them stand up. The tape and supports are changed every week or so, and this procedure may go on for four to six months, until the dog's ears stand up on their own.

Many more breeds are shown with tails that have been artificially shortened, which is called docking. Part of the tail may be surgically removed, or a tight rubber ring may be placed around it, restricting the blood flow. The tail then usually falls off in a few days. More than 50 breeds are shown with docked tails, including most of the spaniels, and many types of terriers.

Also, the issue of just what is and is not a purebred animal is a relatively recent problem for both dogs and cats. Official registries that keep track of the ancestry (called a pedigree) of purebred dogs and cats were founded in the late 1800s and early 1900s. Before that, the breed of an animal was determined by what it looked like and what job it did. If someone raised Labrador Retrievers and wanted them to run

Fluffy Persian cats can develop kidney trouble if not bred properly.

faster, they would be bred to faster dogs, such as Greyhounds. Such puppies would keep the retrieving ability of the Lab and pick up the speed of the Greyhound.

But as working animals became less necessary and dog shows became more popular, looks started to play a more important role than physical abilities. Breeders wanted to establish a certain physical makeup that would distinguish each breed. They wrote breed standards and started registries. These registries keep track of each animal's pedigree. The problem is that the registries are closed; once

CATS NEED THEIR CLAWS

Scratching is a natural and necessary behavior in all cats. If you give them scratching surfaces they like, they'll scratch those. But if you don't, they may scratch your furniture. In the past, people believed a simple solution to unwanted scratching was to declaw a cat. But a growing body of scientific evidence shows that declawing can have serious medical and behavioral consequences for a cat.

Declaw surgery doesn't just remove the cat's claws; the veterinarian cuts off the end of the last bone, which contains the growth plate along the nail. That's like cutting off the ends of your fingers.

Cats use their claws not only to scratch, but also to anchor themselves when they run and climb, steady themselves when they jump, express pleasure, and manipulate objects. All these behaviors are compromised when they no longer have their claws.

Many declawed cats develop changes in their feet that prevent them from walking normally. And the U.S. Centers for Disease Control and Prevention says declawing a cat is not necessary to prevent disease, even in people with weakened immune systems who might be scratched.

Many countries around the world have banned the surgery, including Australia, Belgium, Great Britain, Germany, France, Ireland, Israel, Italy, New Zealand, Portugal, and Spain. And several cities and states in the United States either have banned declawing cats or are considering legislation to ban it.

Labrador retrievers have a natural instinct to work outdoors.

a breed enters the registry, only animals that were in the registry from the beginning can produce offspring that also get registered. If a breed starts out with very few animals in the registry, they must all be bred to one another again and again. The gene pool is therefore very small.

Among cats, some breeds began with just a single cat born with an unusual characteristic, such as a curly coat or an unusual shape to the ears. These breeds allow **outcrossing** to keep the breed healthy. But the extent of the outcrossing is limited, and the gene pool is still very small.

Testing the Gene Pool

Breeders try to make up for this small gene pool by not breeding animals that have genetic health problems. For example, epilepsy can be genetic. If you have an epileptic cat and you don't breed her, those genes will not be passed on.

The problem is that some genes are dominant, which means every animal carrying those genes will have what that gene controls. But some genes are recessive, which means you must have two copies of the gene (one from each parent) to get the same result. So an animal could be carrying a recessive gene and seem perfectly healthy, but if you bred her to another healthy animal with the same recessive gene, the offspring would have a health problem—and there's no way you could predict or avoid that. Even with diseases that are caused by dominant genes, sometimes the disease does not show up until the animal is older.

Breeders are working with researchers to develop genetic tests for diseases, so that affected animals can be identified before they are bred. But only a handful of tests have been developed so far.

Another problem is that not all breeders are so careful about the animals they breed. Breeders who show their animals in dog and cat shows typically use all the tests available to them and study pedigree information to try to avoid breeding animals that might carry unhealthy genes. But the majority of purebred dogs and cats are bred by commercial breeders, who just want to breed as many animals as possible to make a profit. They make sure the animals are purebred, but they don't worry about passing on health problems.

For all these reasons, mixed-breed dogs and cats are said to be much healthier than purebred animals. Breeders have claimed this is not so, but a 2013 study published in the *Journal of the American Veterinary Medical Association* found that it is often true, at least for dogs. The study looked at the medical records of more than 27,000 dogs and compared how many mixed-breed dogs and how many

"What's wrong with a mutt?" these shelter dogs ask owners.

purebred dogs developed one of 24 health problems that are known to be inherited. The researchers found that 10 of those genetic disorders occurred significantly more often in purebred dogs, and just one of those disorders occurred more often in mixed-breed dogs. The remaining disorders occurred at about the same rate in both groups.

Purebred vs. mutt

TEXT-DEPENDENT QUESTIONS

1. What are brachycephalic breeds? Name one or two of those breeds.

2. What is the difference between dominant and recessive genes?

3. What procedure for cats is banned in many countries, according to the text?

RESEARCH PROJECT

Pick a favorite dog or cat breed and research its pedigree. Look online to find out how far back the line goes. What characteristics does the breed have? Which ones can you find that have changed or been refined over time?

WORDS TO UNDERSTAND

chronic   an illness that lasts for a long time

domesticated   a tame animal that is kept as a pet or on a farm

forage   to search widely for food

reactive   easily shows a strong reaction to something

POSITIVE TRAINING

Imagine you have been kidnapped by giant aliens who take you to their planet. There, everything is unfamiliar and is built for them and their big, slow, unathletic bodies. None of them speak your language. They want you to behave in a certain way and follow rules, so they try to teach you what they want.

Every time you do something they don't like, they shout and hit you. You don't really know how they want you to behave, so the hits seem to come at random times. Eventually you figure out the pattern and you are able to follow their rules. But you do it because you're afraid of getting hit, not because you are happy to cooperate with them. You don't enjoy these lessons.

Now imagine that instead of hitting you when you behave in a way they don't like, they just wait until you behave in a way they do like. When you do, they make a happy noise and give you a potato chip. If you do something they don't like, they either ignore you, or ask you do to something else that you've already learned. That way, it's easy to avoid mistakes! You love potato chips, and you look forward to your lessons so you can earn more of them. You really pay attention and put a lot of effort into learning.

This is what training feels like for your pets. There's no need to be the scary alien who punishes them, and, in fact, they will learn more quickly when you're the nice alien who gives out rewards. This is what **behaviorists** call positive training—rewarding desirable behavior and redirecting undesirable behavior.

Training With Encouragement

Studies have shown that when you train using punishment, animals learn more slowly and are less eager to cooperate. They try to escape the punishment, but they don't make any extra effort to cooperate with you. Punishment-based training is also less clear for the animal. Why would that be so?

appropriate behaviors, not rewarding undesired behaviors, and clearly and consistently communicating how you want your pet to behave. Positive training leads to voluntary co-operation, not dominance.

Protecting our dog and cat pets means taking care of the ones that are part of our families, while working with groups that are trying to deal with the issue of too many homeless animals. The best thing for a pet owner is to make sure their dog or cat is well cared for, providing the right food, the right amount of exercise, and, of course, lots of love.

TEXT-DEPENDENT QUESTIONS

1. Why does a spray bottle rarely work to train cats?
2. Describe clicker training.
3. What does the author say about the "dominance myth"?

RESEARCH PROJECT

Do you have a pet? Read more about clicker training and give it a shot. If it works well, arrange a demonstration for your class.

Adopt your pet. If you have your heart set on a particular breed, adopt from a breed rescue group. Or find a small hobby breeder who raises the puppies or kittens at home and tests the animals for inherited diseases. Put yourself on a waiting list for the next litter. It will be worth waiting for!

Spay or neuter your pet. There are already more pets available than there are forever homes. Spayed and neutered pets are healthier, more family-oriented, and don't contribute to the homelessness problem.

Make a lifetime commitment.
Animals end up in shelters either because they are picked up as strays, or because their owners take them to a shelter. According to the American Humane Association, the most common

reasons people give up both dogs and cats is because where they live doesn't allow pets. When you adopt a pet, make a commitment to keep that pet with you, no matter where you move. You can find pet-friendly housing everywhere.

Keep your pet at a good weight. Our pets can't feed themselves, so if they're overweight, it's because we've fed them too much. Choose a high-quality food and your pet will need less of it. Cats and dogs lose weight the same way people lose weight: eat less, make smart food choices, and exercise more. Ask your veterinarian for guidance on the best foods for your pet.

Train positively. Show off your well-trained dog or cat, and explain to others how positive training makes the process fun and easy.

Volunteer to help. Whatever you like to do, there's a group that needs help doing it. You can play with the animals, walk the dogs, kiss the cats, make toys for the puppies and kittens, or help organize a fundraiser. You can also help take care of a feral cat colony.

FIND OUT MORE

BOOKS:

Bradshaw, John, and Sarah Ellis. **The Trainable Cat.** New York: Basic Books, 2016.

Bradshaw, John. **Dog Sense.** New York: Basic Books, 2014.

Delzio, Suzanne, and Cindy Ribarich, DVM. **Felinestein: Pampering the Genius in Your Cat.** New York: HarperCollins, 1999.

Johnson-Bennett, Pam. **Think Like a Cat.** New York: Penguin, 2011.

Stilwell, Victoria. **Train Your Dog Positively.** Emeryville, CA: Ten Speed Press, 2013.

WEBSITES:

apdt.com/pet-owners/
The Association of Professional Dog Trainers has training and behavior information for dog owners, as well as tips on how to choose a great dog trainer.

indoorpet.osu.edu
The Indoor Pet Initiative has great information about creating an enriching home environment for dogs and cats, positive training, and ways to change unwanted behavior. It's run by the Ohio State University College of Veterinary Medicine.

pets.webmd.com
WebMD has a great section devoted to dogs and cats. It has information on basic care, health, and behavior.

acidification the process of making something have a higher acid concentration, a process happening now to world oceans

activist someone who works for a particular cause or issue

biodiverse having a large variety of plants and animals in a particular area

ecosystem the places where many species live, and how they interact with each other and their environment

habitat the type of area a particular type of animal typically lives in, with a common landscape, climate, and food sources

keystone a part of a system that everything else depends on

poaching illegally killing protected or privately-owned animals

pollination the process of fertilizing plants, often accomplished by transferring pollen from plant to plant

sustain to keep up something over a long period of time

toxin a poison

INDEX

PHOTO CREDITS

ABOUT THE AUTHOR

Beth Adelman, MS, is a cat behavior consultant, a member of the Pet Professional Guild, and the former editor of *Cats* magazine and *DogWorld*. She lives in Brooklyn with her husband and three well-trained cats.